An Old Fashioned MERRY FUCKING CHRISTMAS

A Swearing Adult Coloring Book For The Holidays

All vintage images are from the British Library on-line collection
found at www.flickr.com/photos/britishlibrary

instagram

Post coloring pages on instagram @colormenaughtybooks
#merryfuckingchristmas

OTHER BOOKS BY COLOR ME NAUGHTY

 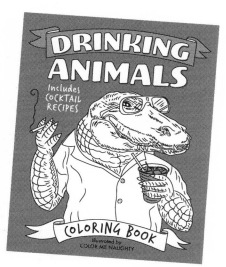

Copyright © 2018 by Color Me Naughty

ISBN: 9781731359001

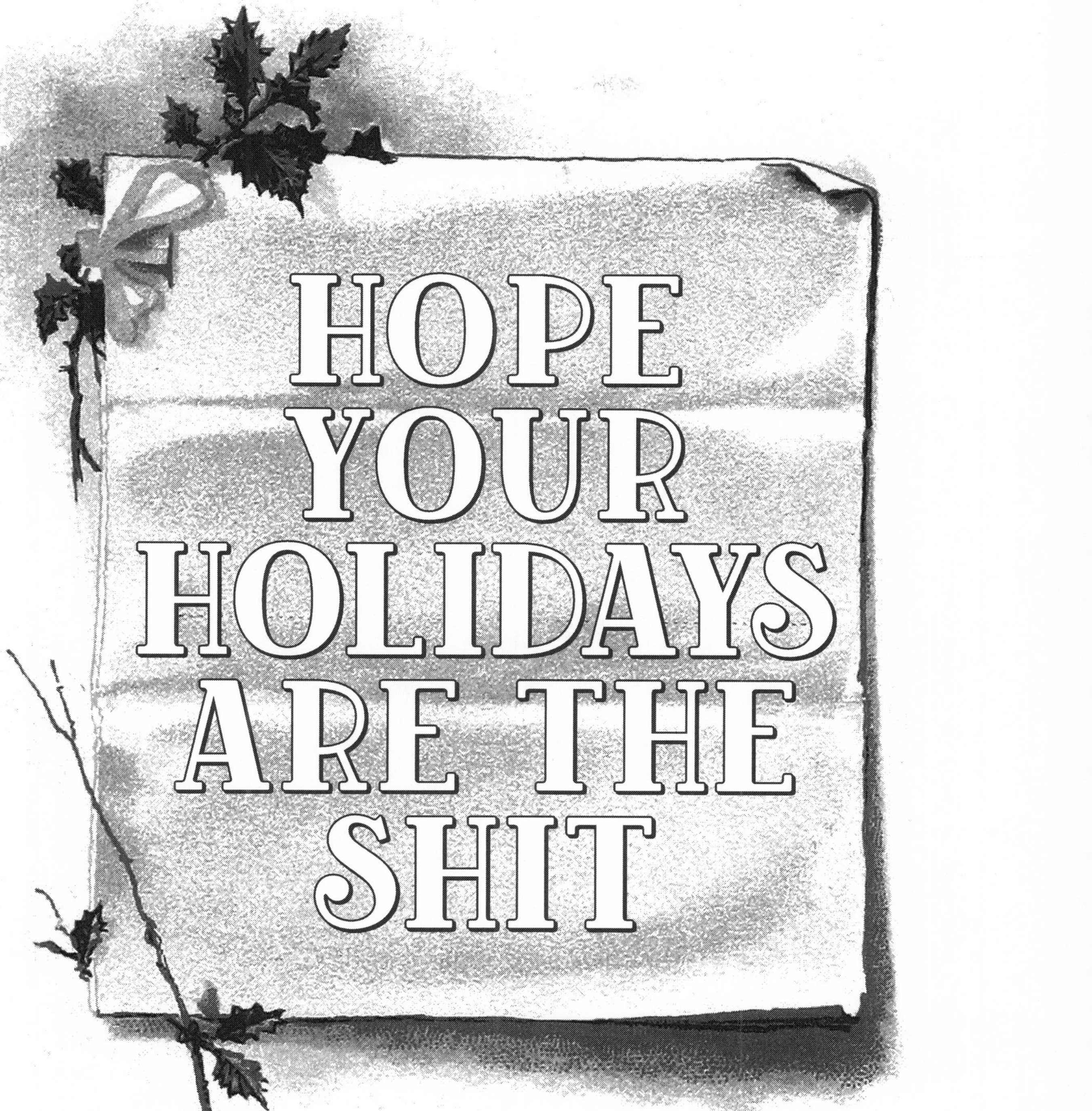
HOPE
YOUR
HOLIDAYS
ARE THE
SHIT

COLORED BY

DATE

HAVE YOURSELF A MERRY FUCKING CHRISTMAS

COLORED BY

DATE

IT'S BEGINNING TO LOOK A LOT LIKE FUCK THIS

COLORED BY

DATE

COLORED BY

....

DATE

....

DECK THE
FUCKING HALLS
YOURSELF

COLORED BY

DATE

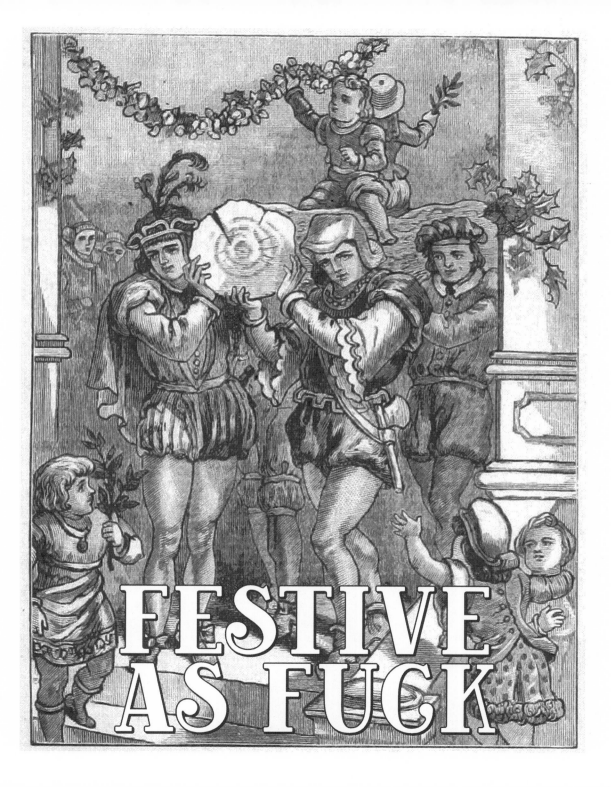

COLORED BY

DATE

CHEER UP YOU GRUMPY BITCHES, IT'S CHRISTMAS

COLORED BY

DATE

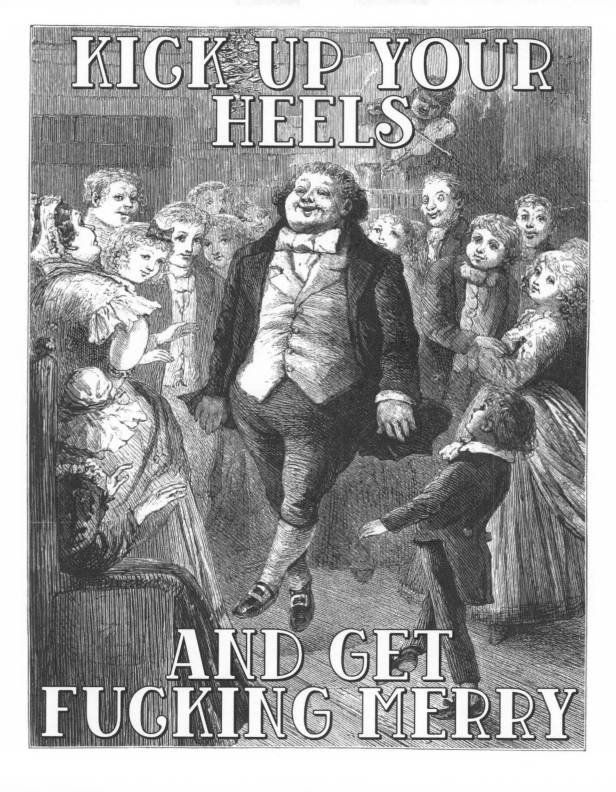

COLORED BY

DATE

COLORED BY

DATE

FUCK OFF.
I MEAN,
MERRY CHRISTMAS.

COLORED BY

DATE

KICK THIS
HOLIDAY IN ITS
GLITTERING ASS

COLORED BY

....

DATE

....

DID I ASK YOUR FUCKING OPINION ABOUT MY HOLIDAY DECOR?

COLORED BY

....

DATE

....

DARLING...LET'S SPEND LOADS OF MONEY ON SHIT WE DON'T NEED.

COLORED BY

....

DATE

....

COLORED BY

DATE

BAH
FUCKING
HUMBUG

COLORED BY

....

DATE

....

GET THE HELL OUT
OF MY KITCHEN

COLORED BY

....

DATE

....

BITCH NO, I HAVEN'T FINISHED MY FUCKING CHRISTMAS SHOPPING.

COLORED BY

DATE

MERRY CHRISTMAS.
JUST KIDDING,
GO FUCK
YOURSELF.

COLORED BY

....

DATE

....

COLORED BY

DATE

HO HO HOLY SHIT
IT'S CHRISTMAS

COLORED BY

DATE

MERRY CHRISTMAS AND ALL THAT SHIT

COLORED BY

....

DATE

....

YOU'RE NOT GETTING JACK SHIT THIS YEAR

COLORED BY

DATE

COLORED BY

....

DATE

....

WISHING YOU A SHITLOAD OF HAPPINESS THIS HOLIDAY SEASON

COLORED BY

DATE

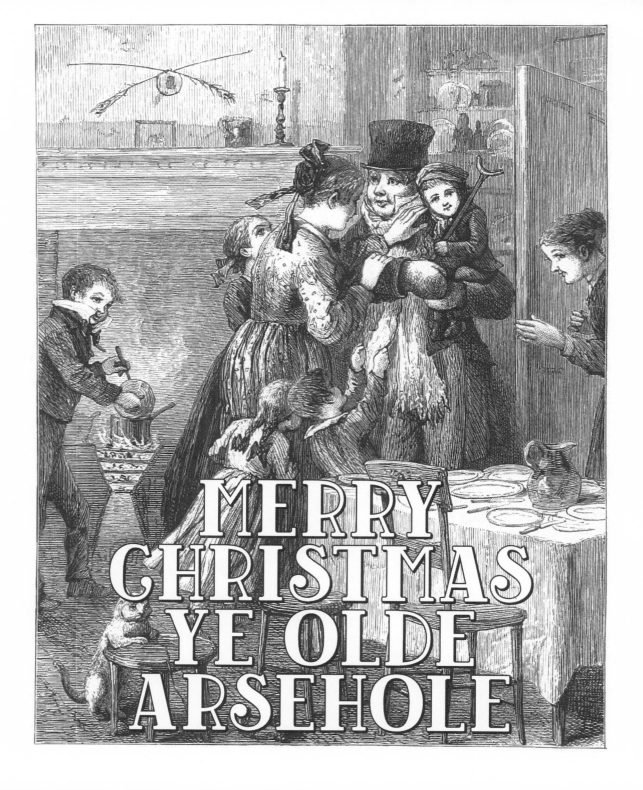

COLORED BY

....

DATE

....

THIS IS A BUNCH
OF CUTE BULLSHIT

COLORED BY

....

DATE

....

COLORED BY

DATE

CUTE LITTLE FUCKERS

COLORED BY

DATE

COLORED BY

....

DATE

....

YOU'RE GETTING FUCK-ALL FROM SANTA

COLORED BY

DATE

COLORED BY

DATE

COLORED BY

....

DATE

....

COLORED BY

....

DATE

....

NO, I DON'T WANT
TO BUILD A
FUCKING SNOWMAN

COLORED BY

....

DATE

....

JUST BE FUCKING MERRY

COLORED BY

....

DATE

....

Made in the USA
Middletown, DE
09 December 2019